Let's Talk About
TATTLING

Let's Talk About

TATTLING

By JOY BERRY

Illustrated by John Costanza

Edited by Orly Kelly

Designed by Jill Losson

GROLIER ENTERPRISES CORP.

Let's talk about TATTLING.

TATTLING is telling a secret about another person.

Sometimes tattling can hurt the other person. Oftentimes it gets the other person into trouble.

Some people tattle because they want *attention*. They think that tattling will get someone to notice them.

But tattling will not get you the kind of attention you want or need.

Thus, you should not tattle to get attention.

Some people tattle to make themselves *seem better* than others. They want to make other people appear to be bad so that they will appear to be good.

But tattling will not make you seem better.

Thus, you should not tattle to make someone think that you are good.

Some people tattle because they are too *lazy* to solve their own problems. They want another person to solve their problems for them.

But it is best that you solve your own problems if possible. Thus, you should not ask anyone to help you solve a problem that you can solve yourself.

Some people tattle because they want to *hurt* other people. They want to get other people into trouble.

But you should never do anything to hurt another person.

Thus, you should not tattle on someone just to cause trouble.

Too much tattling may bother the people you are tattling to. They may become annoyed and get angry with you.

Tattling will most likely upset
the person you are tattling on. He
or she may get angry with you and
not want to be around you.

Thus, tattling can harm you and the people around you.

This does not mean that you should never tattle.

If a person's life is in danger, you must tell someone.

To know whether you should tattle,
ask yourself: "Am I tattling because
I want to help someone, or am I tattling
to hurt someone?"

If you are tattling to help someone, do it.

If you are tattling to hurt someone, don't
do it.

Before you tattle, you should ask yourself a second question: "Have I done everything I can to help solve the problem?"

You should not tattle unless you have done all you can to help solve the problem.

It is important to treat other people
the way you want to be treated.

If you see someone doing something wrong,
think of how you would want to be
treated if you were that person.

Try to understand why the other person
is doing what he or she is doing.
Help the other person to do what is right
if help is needed.

You probably don't like it when people tattle on you. Thus, you should try not to tattle on other people.

It is best if you tattle only when
someone's life or property is in danger.

You should tattle to help people not to hurt
themselves or to help protect their property.